Beautiful Lakes
For Kids!

Nature Books for Kids
By
K. Bennett and John Davidson

JD-Biz Publishing

Read More Amazing Animal Books

Table of Contents

Introduction

*All water has a perfect memory and is forever trying to get back to where it was~ **Toni Morrison***

***

Lakes: Lakes are beautiful bodies of water found on earth. They are fun to explore and fun to learn about.

Lots of interesting creatures live in lakes and you can find cool plants that live around them too.

What do you know about lakes? Have you ever visited or explored one?

Let's learn more!

Lakes have been around for a very long time and there are many different kinds. Did you know some lakes are formed when Volcanoes explode? Some are formed when glaciers melt, and some are born when underground plates called "tectonic plates" move around!

If you think of a lake what shape comes to your mind? Did you think of a circle or something like a circle? In the case of a lake, this shape is called a **basin** and they look like a big bowl of water!

Lakes are all over the planet, in all shapes and sizes. National Geographic estimates the earth has several million. That's a lot of lakes! Can you guess where lakes might be found?

All the continents in the World have lakes.

If you go to the mountains, you will find them. If you hop over the desert you will find them too! What about by the seashore? Yes! They are there and even the plains have lakes.

Some lakes are very small and they are called ponds. Other lakes are very large, we call them seas.

Some lakes are very shallow. Other lakes are very deep, like Lake Baikal in Russia. If you decide to dive down into the water, it will take you more than a mile to get to the bottom! Do you know how many feet are in a mile?

5,280 feet!

Or if you prefer to measure in kilometers the lake is almost 2 kilometers deep. That's a very deep lake!

Some lakes are way up in the mountains like Lake Titicaca. This beautiful lake is found at 12,500 feet above sea level!

Strange animals live around the lake like giant frogs. This place is also called the "Birthplace of the Incas" and is full of lots of interesting stories. I will tell you about one of them at the end of this book.

Other lakes are not as high as Lake Titicaca. The Dead Sea is the lowest lake in the world! Pretty neat, don't you think? But how low is it?

1,300 feet *below* sea level!

As you can see, lakes are amazing bodies of water and really cool to explore. But there are lots more we can learn about them.

So…if you are ready, let's dive into the wonderful world of lakes!

(Source: http://education.nationalgeographic.com/encyclopedia/lake/)

DID YOU KNOW?

Many people love to explore and study lakes as a hobby. This is called **LIMNOLOGY**.

Chapter 1

Let's Explore!

Ok Explorer! Let's find out what lakes are all about.

What is a Lake?

It is water surrounded on all sides, by land.

So water is a very important part of what makes a lake. Without water, can you call it a lake? What do you think?

Kidsgeo.com says that 90% of all the water in the world is found in lakes, this does not include the sea!

The interesting thing about lakes is how it gets water. Do you think lakes can produce their own water? Yes or no? If your answer is yes, do you know how? And if your answer is no, do you know why not?

The truth is lakes need to have a water source. This simply means they need to get their water from somewhere else. A river or a stream, is an example of where a lake might get it's water. And if a lake does not get water, it will dry up and disappear!

This can take a long time to happen and in some cases, it takes thousands of years. But a lake cannot be a lake without a constant source of water! Makes sense?

Now that we know exactly what a lake is, let's find out about the different types of lakes.

Different types of lakes

Just like people, lakes come in lots of colors, shapes, and sizes! To learn more about them, we will first talk about the **GREAT LAKES**, they hold 6 quadrillion (6,000,000,000,000,000) gallons of water! Wow!!! Isn't that amazing?

The Great Lakes have lots of wonderful things to explore like cool animals and plants! How many species of plants can you find around the Great Lakes?

More than 3,500 different species that live around the Great Lakes!

Lake Superior

This lake has a very "superior" name! But what makes it great is not the name but the water it has. It is one of the biggest bodies of fresh water on planet earth. Some say it is the biggest!

When winter comes around, this lake can get very cold and freeze. It doesn't usually freeze completely, except it did in 1997 and 2003. It may freeze all over in the future too. We will have to wait and see.

Lots of fish live in Lake Superior. Around 80 species of fish and lots of plants grow there too. Did you know there are about 60 species of Orchids around the lake?

But these are not the only wonders you will find. If you were to visit the lake, you might hear owls hooting or see hawks flying high. You might even hear the woodpeckers pecking away or the sound of migrating birds.

Lake Huron

Does the name Huron sound like an Indian name to you? That's because it is! This name comes from the Wyandot Indians, also called Hurons, they lived around the lake. This lake has a very beautiful shore and lots of people love to visit during the summer. Why? Because the water is very nice to swim in!

This lake does not freeze like Lake Superior. Lots of fish swim in the waters like: yellow perch, walleye, smallmouth bass, white bass, and more.

Lake Huron has many beautiful pinewood trees, that are protected, thanks to in being in the Manistee National Forest.

Lake Erie

Lake Erie is shaped like a long tail and that is where it gets the name "Erie," which is Iroquian for "long tail!" This lake is warmer than the other lakes but it can freeze too!

There is something very interesting about this lake. Did you know a great battle was fought here in 1812? It was the battle between the U.S. Navy and the British Navy. Who won the fight? Why don't you research a little bit of history to find the answer?

Lake Ontario

This lake is very close to Niagara with lots of lagoons. Lake Ontario is very important in history especially after the fighting in 1812 between the U.S. and the British Navy.

Lots of steamships traveled across the waters with their bright wheels and pretty colors.

Lots of salmon swim around the lake like Chinook and Coho salmon. Migratory birds also visit the lake and many fruit trees are grown in the area like pears, plums, apples, and cherries. Yum! Yum!

Lake Michigan

This lake is very special. Unlike the other great lakes, this is the only one entirely in the United States. It was discovered in 1634 by a French Explorer named Samuel Champlain. He must have been very excited to see such a beautiful body of water!

Lake Michigan has a very interesting personality. Sometimes it is calm and sometimes it can be quite rough! It can be very hard to ride the waves when the lake isn't feeling too happy!

Lots of wildlife lives around Lake Michigan. The tall grass prairies, marshes, and forests are great places for all sorts of creatures to call home!

(*Source:* http://www.livescience.com/29312-great-lakes.html)

Did you enjoy learning about the Great Lakes? Wonderful! There are many other lakes on the planet, so I invite you to explore and see what else you can discover!

Don't forget to ask your parent or a guardian's permission before you search.

COOL FACTS FOR KIDS:

There are many islands in the world but only one of them has a freshwater island, it is found in Lake Huron! This island is called the "Heart and Spirit of the Great Lakes."

Manitoulin Island is a very special place and in the native Ojibwe language, it means "God's Island."

Chapter 2

Lakes are Amazing!

Now that you know a little about Lakes, let's see what other treasures we can discover about some of them!

Dead Sea - Jordan

Not all lakes are Freshwater lakes. Some of them are full of salt like the Dead Sea. Scientists say the Dead Sea is the saltiest lake in the world!

It is even saltier than the Ocean so many people call it "the salt sea," instead of the Dead Sea.

This lake is very low and falls $1,388$ feet below sea level.

Lots of interesting formations like salt deposits are found in the lake and if you wanted to swim you would float very easily because of the high salt found in the water! *National Geographic* says it has 10 times more salt than the Ocean but guess what? It is getting saltier all the time!

The salt is so high that many creatures can't live there except for some types of bacteria and fungi.

What do you think? Would you like the visit the Dead Sea or would you prefer to visit the "land of a thousand lakes?"

Lake Saiima - Finland

Finland is a country with so many lakes it is called the "land of a thousand lakes." More than $100,000$ lakes are found in Finland. That's a lot of lakes, don't you think?

Of all the lakes in the world, Lake Saiima is the only place you can find the Saiima ringed seal. This creature is very beautiful but endangered.

Scientist say Lake Saiima was formed when the glaciers melted and it is the biggest lake in Finland!

Caspian Sea

The Caspian Sea is very special because it is a sea and a lake! You might be curious to know why it is called a sea and a lake. Well, the Romans called it a Sea because it was so big and today we call it both a Sea and a lake!

The water in the Caspian Sea is salty but not nearly as salty as the Dead Sea! Lots of islands are in the sea but many of them don't have people living there.

There is a special fish that lives in the Caspian Sea called a Sturgeon. Their eggs are used to make Caviar!

FUN FACTS FOR KIDS:

There are lots of different words we use when talking about Lakes or bodies of water. Words like: Evolve, Craters, Marsh, Isolated, Salt marsh, Swamp, Channel, Loch, Reservoir and more! Do you know what these words mean? Look at the definition to see the meaning of the words.

-*Evolve:* Changes over time or adapts to new conditions.

-*Craters:* Big, deep round holes.

-*Marsh:* Wet area with lots of plants.

-*Isolated*: Far away from others or out of the way.

-*Salt Marsh:* Flat land where salt water flows over

-*Swamp:* Low land that seasonally floods with lots of woody plants.

-*Channel:* A passage where waters flows through

-*Loch:* Is another name for a body of water in Scotland. Some lakes are also called lochs but not all of them! Have you ever heard of the loch nest monster?

-*Reservoir:* An artificial lake made by humans or manmade lake!

Chapter 3

More Fun facts!

Now let's talk about some cool facts about lakes. Ready?

- Do you remember what a **reservoir** is? Good job! Many lakes are reservoirs and used to make Hydro Electric Power! The word Hydro come from water and you already know what electric means. I am guessing you know what power means too!

So, Hydro Electric Power simply means: Water power or Water energy! Many people get their electricity this way. In the year 2006 around 20% of the energy in the world came from Hydro Electric Power! Some countries use this type of energy a lot like: New Zealand, Brazil, Venezuela, Norway, Paraguay, and Canada.

Canada is a country with lots of different lakes. There are over 2 million lakes in Canada! Do you know about any of them? Here is a small list:

1-Great Bear Lake

2-Reindeer Lake

3-Southern Indian Lake

4-Lake Manitoba

5-Lake Winnipeg

6-Baker Lake

7-Cedar Lake

8-Island Lake

9-Cree Lake

10-Kasba Lake

-Why don't you pick a name and see what else you can learn about Canada's lakes?

Lots of water activities happen in or around a lake! Activities like: Water skiing, cruising, sailing, swimming, kayaking, jet skiing, fishing, diving, feeding the ducks or just enjoying a nice picnic with family and friends!

Although lakes are very beautiful, they can get very ugly too! How? Pollution and acid rain can destroy a beautiful lake and the animals that live in it. Acid rain is a real problem in the world today. Do you know what acid rain is?

Acid rain:

This only means polluted rain or rain that has bad particles in it. Where does the rain get the bad particles? From planet earth!

The gas that comes from factories, cars, and even homes is not very good. This type of gas is an acid gas and it goes into the sky!

When these gases mix with rain or snow or fog and it comes back to earth, it becomes acid rain. This type of rain hurts the lakes and even kills the animals. It is also true that lots of gases go into the atmosphere when volcanoes blow their top!

What kind of gas causes acid rain?

Clean-air-kids.org says the gases are primarily sulphur and nitrogen. When these gases get into the air and mix with the rain it turns into sulphur dioxide and nitrogen oxides. This is what makes it so bad for the lakes and the creatures inside the water. It's not good for humans either!

How does acid rain affect lakes?

Sadly, acid rain is very bad for water life. It is so bad that in Scandinavia, thousands of beautiful lakes no longer have creatures in it! They have all died because they couldn't live in the water. Even plants died after too much acid rain.

But there is good news! Many people now know what kind of pollutions hurts the planet and they are fighting very hard to make the air clean. What about you? How can you help?

And now for the story I promised you!

Lots of countries have very interesting stories of how life began on planet earth but one of these stories has to do with Lake Titicaca in the Andes.

This lake is very different from other lakes. Do you remember why? Yes! It is very high above sea level. But the story of Lake Titicaca starts with the Inca civilization.

The Incas believed that this place is where humans came from. They said the God Viracocha came out of the lake and made...can you guess what he made first? The sun! Then he made the universe, the stars, and last he made people.

When they painted Viracocha he had thunderbolts in his hands, the sun as a crown on his head, and tears falling from his eyes like the rains from the sky.

Can you guess how he made humans? Legend says he breathed into rocks or stones and then humans started to live. And one day Viracocha decided to travel across the great Pacific Ocean and disappeared! Some say he still walks around the earth dressed like a beggar trying to help people.

What do you think about this story?

Conclusion:

In conclusion: Learning about lakes can be a fun project! Would you like to continue learning a little more about them?

*Here are some more ideas to help you in your lake learning quest.

Choose a lake you would like to learn about and answer the following questions:

-When was it discovered?

-How big is it?

-How deep is it?

-Where is it located?

-What is the temperature?

-What are the good things about the lake?

-What are the bad things about the lake?

-What kind of equipment do you need to explore the lake?

-What kind of clothes do you need to wear?

-Is it great for children and older ones to swim in or only for adults in good physical health?

Another creative idea for you!

Pick a lake, any lake, and think about the best way to protect it. If you were in charge, what would you do to keep the lake clean?

You might like also to visit the National Wildlife Foundation at www.nwf.org.

This foundation is all about protecting planet earth and getting young ones involved in the activities. There is also a nice section about protecting the Great Lakes with tips on what you can do.

More Ideas:

There are lots of interesting animals that live around lakes. Why don't you take a moment and find one for your school project? Choose a mysterious creature and share your findings with your schoolmates and your teacher.

If you don't know which creature to choose, do some research, and find something exciting to talk about.

Fun activity:

There is a neat activity at Kids Crossing that shows how lakes and rivers are formed and how they are connected to a watershed.

To understand how this works, let's try an experiment and this is what you will need:

- A spray bottle filled with water
- A marker
- A sheet of letter size paper (8 ½ x 11)

Steps:

1. Take the piece of paper and crumple it in your hand. When you open it, do not smooth it out because you need the wrinkles in the paper for the activity to work.

2. Hold the paper in the palm of your hand and see what it looks like. The highest wrinkles you see are mountains and the lower wrinkles are valleys.

3. Use your markers and start to draw lines. Put them everywhere you think rivers, creeks and lakes should be! There is no right or wrong answer…just draw the lines wherever you want to draw them.

4. Get the spray bottle and spray the paper. Be very careful not to spray too much water for your paper to get soggy! Just spray enough for the little drops of water to run around and then you will see where the water settles.

Can you see where the water went? Did it go where you expected it to go? What did you learn from this experiment?

This activity teaches you that the flow of water depends on the shape of the ground!

(Source: https://eo.ucar.edu/kids/wwe/lake4.htm)

But wait, I have **another suggestion** for you.

If you would like to be a junior reporter someday do this: Check out some newspapers and see if you can find any stories about lakes. It can be school newspapers or even listening to the radio. Did you hear anything important? If you were giving the report would you have done it the same or would you add other details?

And finally...

If there is someone who knows a lot about water, why don't you interview them and see what good things they have to share? After all: Sharing is caring!

I hope you enjoyed this book on **Beautiful Lakes** and always remember…

"Educating the mind without educating the heart is no education at all." - *Aristotle*

Author Bio

K. Bennett loves to write for both children and adults. Many different subjects are interesting to develop, but writing for children is special to her heart.

Her favorite pastimes include reading, traveling and discovering new things. Each of these activities helps to fuel her imagination and acts like a blank canvas waiting for more stories.

She is intrigued with fantasy elements like hidden worlds and faraway lands. And basically anything that gets her imagination soaring to new heights!

Her writing credits include children books online and other writing works listed at Amazon.com

Our books are available at

1. Amazon.com

2. Barnes and Noble

3. Itunes

4. Kobo

5. Smashwords

6. Google Play Books

Publisher

JD-Biz Corp

P O Box 374

Mendon, Utah 84325

http://www.jd-biz.com/

Read more books from John Davidson

Amazon.com Author Link

www.ingramcontent.com/pod-product-compliance
Lightning Source LLC
Chambersburg PA
CBHW050850290526
45792CB00002B/595